# 940
## SATURDAYS

### Family Activities & a Keepsake Journal

HARLEY A. ROTBART, MD

POTTER STYLE / PUBLISHERS
NEW YORK

SATURDAY **n**o **1** ● / ● /20 ●

_____

_____

_____

_____

_____

_____

_____

_____

_____

_____


SATURDAY **n**o **2** ● / ● /20 ●

_____

_____

_____

_____

_____

_____

_____

_____

_____

_____

SATURDAY № **3** ● / ● /20 ●

_____

_____

_____

_____

_____

_____

_____

_____

_____

_____

SATURDAY № **4** ● / ● /20 ●

_____

_____

_____

_____

_____

_____

_____

_____

_____

_____

SATURDAY № 5 ● / ● /20 ●

SATURDAY № 6 ● / ● /20 ●

SATURDAY № 7 ● / ● /20 ●

_____

_____

_____

_____

_____

_____

_____

_____

_____

SATURDAY № 8 ● / ● /20 ●

_____

_____

_____

_____

_____

_____

_____

_____

_____

SATURDAY nº **9** ● / ● /20 ●

SATURDAY nº **10** ● / ● /20 ●

SATURDAY № **11** ●/●/20●

SATURDAY № **12** ●/●/20●

SATURDAY № **13** ● ● /20 ●

SATURDAY № **14** ● ● /20 ●

SATURDAY № 15 ● / ● /20 ●

SATURDAY № 16 ● / ● /20 ●

SATURDAY № 17 ⬤ / ⬤ /20 ⬤

_____

SATURDAY № 18 ⬤ / ⬤ /20 ⬤

_____

SATURDAY **n??** **19** ● /● /**20** ●

_____

_____

_____

_____

_____

_____

_____

_____

_____

_____


SATURDAY **n??** **20** ● /● /**20** ●

_____

_____

_____

_____

_____

_____

_____

_____

_____

SATURDAY № 21 ● / ● /20 ●

SATURDAY № 22 ● / ● /20 ●

SATURDAY nº 23 ● / ● /20 ●

SATURDAY nº 24 ● / ● /20 ●

SATURDAY № 25 ● / ● /20 ●

_____
_____
_____
_____
_____
_____
_____
_____
_____
_____

SATURDAY № 26 ● / ● /20 ●

_____
_____
_____
_____
_____
_____
_____
_____
_____
_____

SATURDAY № 27 ● / ● /20 ●

_____

_____

_____

_____

_____

_____

_____

_____

_____

_____

SATURDAY № 28 ● / ● /20 ●

_____

_____

_____

_____

_____

_____

_____

_____

_____

SATURDAY № **29** ○ / ○ /20○

SATURDAY № **30** ○ / ○ /20○

SATURDAY № 31 ● / ● /20 ●

SATURDAY № 32 ● / ● /20 ●

SATURDAY **n°** **33**  / /20

SATURDAY **n°** **34**  /20

SATURDAY № **35** ● / ● /20 ●

SATURDAY № **36** ● / ● /20 ●

SATURDAY № 37 ● /● /20 ●

SATURDAY № 38 ● /● /20 ●

SATURDAY № **39** ● / ● /20 ●

SATURDAY № **40** ● / ● /20 ●

SATURDAY nº 41 ⬤ / ⬤ /20 ⬤

SATURDAY nº 42 ⬤ / ⬤ /20 ⬤

SATURDAY **№ 43** ● / ● /20 ●

SATURDAY **№ 44** ● / ● /20 ●

SATURDAY № **45** ● / ● /20 ●

SATURDAY № **46** ● / ● /20 ●

SATURDAY № 47 ● / ● /20 ●

SATURDAY № 48 ● / ● /20 ●

SATURDAY № **49** ● / ● /20 ●

SATURDAY № **50** ● / ● /20 ●

SATURDAY № **51** ● ● /● /**20** ●

_____

_____

_____

_____

_____

_____

_____

_____

_____

_____


SATURDAY № **52** ● ● /● /**20** ●

_____

_____

_____

_____

_____

_____

_____

_____

_____

_____

SATURDAY nº 53 ◯ / ◯ /20 ◯

SATURDAY nº 54 ◯ / ◯ /20 ◯

SATURDAY nº 55 ⬤/⬤/20⬤

SATURDAY nº 56 ⬤/⬤/20⬤

SATURDAY № 57 ● / ● /20 ●

SATURDAY № 58 ● ● / ● /20 ●

SATURDAY №  **59**  ⬤ / ⬤ /20 ⬤

SATURDAY №  **60**  ⬤ / ⬤ /20 ⬤

SATURDAY **n⁰ 61** ⬤ / ⬤ /20 ⬤

SATURDAY **n⁰ 62** ⬤ / ⬤ /20 ⬤

SATURDAY № **63** ●/●/20●

SATURDAY № **64** ●/●/20●

SATURDAY № **65** / /20
SATURDAY № **66** / /20

SATURDAY № **67** ● / ● /20 ●

SATURDAY № **68** ● / ● /20 ●

SATURDAY № **69** ● / ● /20 ●

SATURDAY № **70** ● / ● /20 ●

SATURDAY n.º 71 ● / ● /20 ●

SATURDAY n.º 72 ● / ● /20 ●

SATURDAY № **73** ● / ● /20 ●

SATURDAY № **74** ● / ● /20 ●

SATURDAY n.º 75 ● /● /20●

SATURDAY n.º 76 ● /● /20●

SATURDAY №️ 77 ⬤ / ⬤ /20 ⬤

_____

_____

_____

_____

_____

_____

_____

_____

_____

_____

SATURDAY №️ 78 ⬤ / ⬤ /20 ⬤

_____

_____

_____

_____

_____

_____

_____

_____

_____

SATURDAY n.º 79 ● / ● /20 ●

_____

_____

_____

_____

_____

_____

_____

_____

_____

_____


SATURDAY n.º 80 ● / ● /20 ●

_____

_____

_____

_____

_____

_____

_____

_____

_____

_____

SATURDAY **n**.**81**  ● ● /● /**20** ●

_____

SATURDAY **n**.**82**  ● ● /● /**20** ●

_____

SATURDAY № 83 ● / ● /20 ●

SATURDAY № 84 ● / ● /20 ●

SATURDAY № 85 ● / ● /20 ●

SATURDAY № 86 ● / ● /20 ●

SATURDAY № 87 ● / ● /20 ●

SATURDAY № 88 ● / ● /20 ●

SATURDAY № **89** ● / ● /20 ●

SATURDAY № **90** ● / ● /20 ●

SATURDAY № 91 ● / ● / 20 ●

SATURDAY № 92 ● / ● / 20 ●

SATURDAY № 93 ● / ● /20 ●

_____

_____

_____

_____

_____

_____

_____

_____

_____

_____


SATURDAY № 94 ● / ● /20 ●

_____

_____

_____

_____

_____

_____

_____

_____

_____

_____

SATURDAY **nº** 95 ● / ● /20 ●

SATURDAY **nº** 96 ● / ● /20 ●

SATURDAY № 97 ● / ● /20 ●

SATURDAY № 98 ● / ● /20 ●

SATURDAY № 99 ● / ● /20 ●

SATURDAY № 100 ● / ● /20 ●

SATURDAY nº 101 ● / ● /20 ●

SATURDAY nº 102 ● / ● /20 ●

SATURDAY № 103 ● / ● /20 ●

SATURDAY № 104 ● / ● /20 ●

SATURDAY **nº** 105 ● /● /20●

SATURDAY **nº** 106 ● /● /20●

SATURDAY № 107  ● / ● /20 ●

SATURDAY № 108  ● / ● /20 ●

SATURDAY №: 109    /  /20

_____

SATURDAY №: 110    /  /20

_____

SATURDAY № 111 ● / ● /20 ●

_____
_____
_____
_____
_____
_____
_____
_____
_____
_____

SATURDAY № 112 ● / ● /20 ●

_____
_____
_____
_____
_____
_____
_____
_____
_____

SATURDAY № **113** ● / ● /20 ●

SATURDAY № **114** ● / ● /20 ●

SATURDAY № 115 ⬤/⬤/20⬤

SATURDAY № 116 ⬤/⬤/20⬤

SATURDAY №. **117** ● / ● /20 ●

SATURDAY №. **118** ● / ● /20 ●

SATURDAY nº 119 ● / ● /20 ●

_____
_____
_____
_____
_____
_____
_____
_____
_____
_____

SATURDAY nº 120 ● / ● /20 ●

_____
_____
_____
_____
_____
_____
_____
_____
_____
_____

SATURDAY № 121 ⬤ / ⬤ /20 ⬤

SATURDAY № 122 ⬤ / ⬤ /20 ⬤

SATURDAY № **123**  ● / ● /20 ●

SATURDAY № **124**  ● / ● /20 ●

SATURDAY № 125 ●/●/20●

SATURDAY № 126 ●/●/20●

SATURDAY № **127** ●/●/20●

SATURDAY № **128** ●/●/20●

SATURDAY № **129** ⬤/⬤/20⬤

_____

SATURDAY № **130** ⬤/⬤/20⬤

_____

SATURDAY **n?** **131** ● / ● /20 ●

SATURDAY **n?** **132** ● / ● /20 ●

SATURDAY № 133 ● / ● /20 ●

SATURDAY № 134 ● / ● /20 ●

SATURDAY № **135** ● /● /20 ●

SATURDAY № **136** ● /● /20 ●

SATURDAY № 137 ●/●/20●

SATURDAY № 138 ●/●/20●

SATURDAY no 139 ● / ● /20 ●

SATURDAY no 140 ● / ● /20 ●

SATURDAY n⁰ **141** ● / ● /20 ●

SATURDAY n⁰ **142** ● / ● /20 ●

SATURDAY № **143** ⬤ / ⬤ /**20** ⬤

SATURDAY № **144** ⬤ / ⬤ /**20** ⬤

SATURDAY **n.º** 145 ● / ● /20 ●

SATURDAY **n.º** 146 ● / ● /20 ●

SATURDAY № 147 ◦ / ◦ /20 ◦

SATURDAY № 148 ◦ / ◦ /20 ◦

SATURDAY № **149** ● / ● /20 ●

_____

_____

_____

_____

_____

_____

_____

_____

_____

_____

SATURDAY № **150** ● / ● /20 ●

_____

_____

_____

_____

_____

_____

_____

_____

_____

_____

SATURDAY № 151 ⬤/⬤/20⬤

SATURDAY № 152 ⬤/⬤/20⬤

SATURDAY № 153 ●/●/20●

SATURDAY № 154 ●●/20●

SATURDAY № 155 ⬤ / ⬤ /20 ⬤

SATURDAY № 156 ⬤ / ⬤ /20 ⬤

SATURDAY № 157 ● / ● /20 ●

SATURDAY № 158 ● / ● /20 ●

SATURDAY № **159**  ⬤ / ⬤ /20 ⬤

SATURDAY № **160**  ⬤ / ⬤ /20 ⬤

SATURDAY №. 161 ● / ● /20 ●

SATURDAY №. 162 ● / ● /20 ●

SATURDAY № 163 ● / ● /20 ●

SATURDAY № 164 ● / ● /20 ●

SATURDAY № 165 ● / ● /20 ●

SATURDAY № 166 ● ● / ● /20 ●

SATURDAY № 167 ● / ● /20 ●

SATURDAY № 168 ● / ● /20 ●

SATURDAY № 169 ⬤ / ⬤ /20 ⬤

SATURDAY № 170 ⬤ / ⬤ /20 ⬤

SATURDAY №. 173 ⬤ / ⬤ /20 ⬤

SATURDAY №. 174 ⬤ / ⬤ /20 ⬤

SATURDAY № 175 ● / ● /20 ●

SATURDAY № 176 ● / ● /20 ●

SATURDAY n.º 177 ● /● /20 ●

SATURDAY n.º 178 ● /● /20 ●

SATURDAY № 179 ● / ● /20●

SATURDAY № 180 ● / ● /20●

SATURDAY № 181 ● /● /20 ●

SATURDAY № 182 ● /● /20 ●

SATURDAY № 183 ● / ● /20 ●

SATURDAY № 184 ● / ● /20 ●

SATURDAY № 185 ● / ● /20 ●

SATURDAY № 186 ● / ● /20 ●

SATURDAY № **187** ⬤/⬤/20⬤

SATURDAY № **188** ⬤/⬤/20⬤

SATURDAY № 189 ● / ● /20 ●

SATURDAY № 190 ● / ● /20 ●

SATURDAY № 191 ● / ● /20 ●

SATURDAY № 192 ● / ● /20 ●

SATURDAY № 193 ● / ● /20 ●

SATURDAY № 194 ● / ● /20 ●

SATURDAY № 195 ● / ● /20 ●

SATURDAY № 196 ● / ● /20 ●

SATURDAY № **197** ● / ● /20 ●

SATURDAY № **198** ● / ● /20 ●

SATURDAY №199 ●/●/20●

SATURDAY №200 ●/●/20●

SATURDAY nº 201  ● /● /20 ●

SATURDAY nº 202  ● /● /20 ●

SATURDAY № 203    ● / ● /20 ●

_____

_____

_____

_____

_____

_____

_____

_____

_____


SATURDAY № 204    ● / ● /20 ●

_____

_____

_____

_____

_____

_____

_____

_____

_____

SATURDAY **nº** 205  ● / ● /20 ●

SATURDAY **nº** 206  ● / ● /20 ●

SATURDAY № 207 ●/●/20●

SATURDAY № 208 ●/●/20●

SATURDAY № 209 ● / ● /20 ●

SATURDAY № 210 ● / ● /20 ●

SATURDAY № 211 ● / ● /20 ●

SATURDAY № 212 ● / ● /20 ●

SATURDAY № 213 ● /● /20●

SATURDAY № 214 ● /● /20●

SATURDAY № **215** ● / ● /20 ●

SATURDAY № **216** ● / ● /20 ●

SATURDAY № 217 ● /● /20 ●

SATURDAY № 218 ● /● /20 ●

SATURDAY № 219 ● / ● /20 ●

SATURDAY № 220 ● / ● /20 ●

SATURDAY nº 221 ● / ● /20 ●

SATURDAY nº 222 ● / ● /20 ●

SATURDAY n° 223 ◐ / ◑ /20 ●

SATURDAY n° 224 ◐ / ◑ /20 ●

SATURDAY № 225 ● /● /20 ●

SATURDAY № 226 ● /● /20 ●

SATURDAY № 227 ● /● /20 ●

_____
_____
_____
_____
_____
_____
_____
_____
_____
_____

SATURDAY № 228 ● /● /20 ●

_____
_____
_____
_____
_____
_____
_____
_____
_____
_____

SATURDAY № 229 ● / ● /20 ●

SATURDAY № 230 ● / ● /20 ●

SATURDAY № 231 ● / ● /20 ●

SATURDAY № 232 ● / ● /20 ●

SATURDAY № 233 ● / ● /20 ●

SATURDAY № 234 ● / ● /20 ●

SATURDAY № 235 ⬤ / ⬤ /20 ⬤

SATURDAY № 236 ⬤ / ⬤ /20 ⬤

SATURDAY № 237 ● / ● /20●

SATURDAY № 238 ● / ● /20●

SATURDAY № 239 ● / ● /20 ●

SATURDAY № 240 ● / ● /20 ●

SATURDAY nº 241 ⬤ / ⬤ /20 ⬤

SATURDAY nº 242 ⬤ / ⬤ /20 ⬤

SATURDAY n.º 243 ⬤/⬤/20⬤

SATURDAY n.º 244 ⬤/⬤/20⬤

SATURDAY № **245** ⬤ / ⬤ /20 ⬤

SATURDAY № **246** ⬤ / ⬤ /20 ⬤

SATURDAY n⁰ 247 ● / ● /20 ●

SATURDAY n⁰ 248 ● / ● /20 ●

SATURDAY № 249    / /20

SATURDAY № 250    / /20

SATURDAY № 251 ● / ● /20 ●

SATURDAY № 252 ● / ● /20 ●

SATURDAY № 253 ● / ● /20 ●

SATURDAY № 254 ● / ● /20 ●

SATURDAY № 255 ● / ● /20 ●

SATURDAY № 256 ● / ● /20 ●

SATURDAY nº 257 ● / ● /20 ●

SATURDAY nº 258 ● / ● /20 ●

SATURDAY № 259 ● / ● /20 ●

SATURDAY № 260 ● / ● /20 ●

SATURDAY № **261** ● / ● /20 ●

SATURDAY № **262** ● / ● /20 ●

SATURDAY nº 263 ● /● /20●

SATURDAY nº 264 ● /● /20●

SATURDAY № 265 ● / ● /20 ●

SATURDAY № 266 ● / ● /20 ●

SATURDAY № 267 ⬤ / ⬤ /20 ⬤

SATURDAY № 268 ⬤ / ⬤ /20 ⬤

SATURDAY № 269 ● / ● /20 ●

SATURDAY № 270 ● / ● /20 ●

SATURDAY № 271 ● / ● /20 ●

SATURDAY № 272 ● / ● /20 ●

SATURDAY n.º 273 ● / ● /20 ●

SATURDAY n.º 274 ● ● /20 ●

SATURDAY nº 275 ● / ● /20 ●

SATURDAY nº 276 ● / ● /20 ●

SATURDAY № 277 ● / ● /20 ●

SATURDAY № 278 ● / ● /20 ●

SATURDAY № 279 ● / ● /20 ●

SATURDAY № 280 ● / ● /20 ●

SATURDAY № 281 ● / ● /20 ●

SATURDAY № 282 ● / ● /20 ●

SATURDAY № 283 ● / ● /20 ●

SATURDAY № 284 ● / ● /20 ●

SATURDAY № 285 ● / ● /20 ●

SATURDAY № 286 ● / ● /20 ●

SATURDAY №: 287 ● / ● /20 ●

SATURDAY №: 288 ● ● / ● /20 ●

SATURDAY № 289  ● / ● /20 ●

SATURDAY № 290  ● / ● /20 ●

SATURDAY n.º 291 ● / ● /20 ●

SATURDAY n.º 292 ● / ● /20 ●

SATURDAY n.º 293 ● / ● /20 ●

SATURDAY n.º 294 ● / ● /20 ●

SATURDAY № 295 ● / ● /20 ●

SATURDAY № 296 ● / ● /20 ●

SATURDAY №: 297 ● / ● /20 ●

SATURDAY №: 298 ● / ● /20 ●

SATURDAY № 299 ● /● /20●

SATURDAY № 300 ● /● /20●

SATURDAY № 301 ⬤ / ⬤ /20 ⬤

SATURDAY № 302 ⬤ / ⬤ /20 ⬤

SATURDAY № 303 ● / ● /20 ●

SATURDAY № 304 ● / ● /20 ●

SATURDAY № **305** ● / ● /20 ●

SATURDAY № **306** ● / ● /20 ●

SATURDAY № 307 ● /● /20 ●

SATURDAY № 308 ● /● /20 ●

SATURDAY № 309 ● / ● /20 ●

SATURDAY № 310 ● / ● /20 ●

SATURDAY № 311 ⬤ / ⬤ /20 ⬤

SATURDAY № 312 ⬤ / ⬤ /20 ⬤

SATURDAY № 313 ● / ● /20 ●

SATURDAY № 314 ● / ● /20 ●

SATURDAY № 315 ● / ● /20 ●

SATURDAY № 316 ● / ● /20 ●

SATURDAY №317 ● /● /20 ●

SATURDAY №318 ● /● /20 ●

SATURDAY № 319 ● / ● /20 ●

SATURDAY № 320 ● / ● /20 ●

SATURDAY n.º 321 ●/●/20●

SATURDAY n.º 322 ●/●/20●

SATURDAY №  323  ● / ● /20 ●

SATURDAY №  324  ● / ● /20 ●

SATURDAY № **325** ● / ● /20 ●

SATURDAY № **326** ● / ● /20 ●

SATURDAY № 327 ● / ● /20 ●

SATURDAY № 328 ● / ● /20 ●

SATURDAY № 329 ● / ● /20 ●

SATURDAY № 330 ● / ● /20 ●

SATURDAY № 331 ● / ● /20 ●

SATURDAY № 332 ● / ● /20 ●

SATURDAY № 333 ● / ● /20 ●

SATURDAY № 334 ● / ● /20 ●

SATURDAY № 335 ⬤ / ⬤ /20 ⬤

SATURDAY № 336 ⬤ / ⬤ /20 ⬤

SATURDAY № 337 ● / ● /20 ●

SATURDAY № 338 ● / ● /20 ●

SATURDAY № 339 ● / ● /20 ●

SATURDAY № 340 ● / ● /20 ●

SATURDAY № 341 ● / ● /20 ●

SATURDAY № 342 ● / ● /20 ●

SATURDAY № 343 ●/●/20●

SATURDAY № 344 ●/●/20●

SATURDAY № **345** ●/●/20●

SATURDAY № **346** ●/●/20●

SATURDAY № 347 ● / ● /20 ●

SATURDAY № 348 ● / ● /20 ●

SATURDAY № 349 ● / ● /20 ●

SATURDAY № 350 ● / ● /20 ●

SATURDAY № 351 ⬤/⬤/20⬤

SATURDAY № 352 ⬤/⬤/20⬤

SATURDAY Nº 353 ⬤ / ⬤ /20 ⬤

SATURDAY Nº 354 ⬤ / ⬤ /20 ⬤

SATURDAY № 355 ● /● /20 ●

SATURDAY № 356 ● /● /20 ●

SATURDAY № **357** ⬤ / ⬤ /20 ⬤

SATURDAY № **358** ⬤ / ⬤ /20 ⬤

SATURDAY № **359** ● / ● /20 ●

SATURDAY № **360** ● / ● /20 ●

SATURDAY № **361**   ● / ● /20 ●

SATURDAY № **362**   ● / ● /20 ●

SATURDAY № 363 ● / ● /20 ●

SATURDAY № 364 ● / ● /20 ●

SATURDAY nº 365 ● / ● /20 ●

SATURDAY nº 366 ● / ● /20 ●

SATURDAY № 367 ● /● /20 ●

SATURDAY № 368 ● /● /20 ●

SATURDAY № 369 ● / ● /20 ●

SATURDAY № 370 ● / ● /20 ●

SATURDAY №. 371 ● / ● /20 ●

SATURDAY №. 372 ● / ● /20 ●

SATURDAY № 373 ● / ● /20 ●

SATURDAY № 374 ● / ● /20 ●

SATURDAY № 375 ●/●/20●

SATURDAY № 376 ●/●/20●

SATURDAY nº 377 ● / ● /20 ●

SATURDAY nº 378 ● / ● /20 ●

SATURDAY № 379 ● / ● /20 ●

SATURDAY № 380 ● / ● /20 ●

SATURDAY № **381** ● / ● /20 ●

---

SATURDAY № **382** ● / ● /20 ●

SATURDAY № 383  ● / ● /20 ●

SATURDAY № 384  ● / ● /20 ●

SATURDAY № 385 ● / ● /20 ●

SATURDAY № 386 ● / ● /20 ●

SATURDAY **№ 387** ● / ● /20 ●

SATURDAY **№ 388** ● / ● /20 ●

SATURDAY № **389** ◯ / ◯ /20 ◯

SATURDAY № **390** ◯ / ◯ /20 ◯

SATURDAY № 391 ⬤/⬤/20⬤

SATURDAY № 392 ⬤/⬤/20⬤

SATURDAY № **393** ● / ● /20 ●

SATURDAY № **394** ● / ● /20 ●

SATURDAY № 395 ● / ● /20●

SATURDAY № 396 ● / ● /20●

SATURDAY № 397 ● / ● /20 ●

SATURDAY № 398 ● / ● /20 ●

SATURDAY № 399     / /20

SATURDAY № 400     / /20

SATURDAY № 401 ● / ● /20 ●

SATURDAY № 402 ● / ● /20 ●

SATURDAY № 403 ● / ● /20 ●

SATURDAY № 404 ● / ● /20 ●

SATURDAY № 405 ● / ● /20 ●

SATURDAY № 406 ● / ● /20 ●

SATURDAY № 407 ● / ● /20 ●

SATURDAY № 408 ● / ● /20 ●

SATURDAY № 409 ● / ● /20 ●

SATURDAY № 410 ● / ● /20 ●

SATURDAY № 411 ● / ● /20 ●

SATURDAY № 412 ● / ● /20 ●

SATURDAY № 413 ● / ● /20 ●

SATURDAY № 414 ● / ● /20 ●

SATURDAY **nº 415** ● / ● /20 ●

SATURDAY **nº 416** ● / ● /20 ●

SATURDAY № 417 ⬤/⬤/20⬤

SATURDAY № 418 ⬤/⬤/20⬤

SATURDAY № 419 ● / ● /20 ●

SATURDAY № 420 ● / ● /20 ●

SATURDAY № 421 ●/●/20●

SATURDAY № 422 ●/●/20●

SATURDAY № 423 ⬤ / ⬤ /20 ⬤

SATURDAY № 424 ⬤ / ⬤ /20 ⬤

SATURDAY №425 ⬤/⬤/20⬤

SATURDAY №426 ⬤/⬤/20⬤

SATURDAY № **427** ◯ /◯ /20◯

SATURDAY № **428** ◯ /◯ /20◯

SATURDAY № 429 ● / ● /20 ●

SATURDAY № 430 ● / ● /20 ●

SATURDAY № 431 ●/●/20●

SATURDAY № 432 ●/●/20●

SATURDAY № 433 ● / ● /20 ●

SATURDAY № 434 ● / ● /20 ●

SATURDAY № 435 ● / ● /20 ●

SATURDAY № 436 ● / ● /20 ●

SATURDAY № **437** ● /● /20 ●

SATURDAY № **438** ● /● /20 ●

SATURDAY № 439 ● / ● /20 ●

SATURDAY № 440 ● / ● /20 ●

SATURDAY №: 441 ● / ● /20 ●

SATURDAY №: 442 ● / ● /20 ●

SATURDAY № 443 /  /20

SATURDAY № 444 /  /20

SATURDAY № 445 ⬤ / ⬤ /20 ⬤

SATURDAY № 446 ⬤ / ⬤ /20 ⬤

SATURDAY № 447 ● / ● /20 ●

SATURDAY № 448 ● / ● /20 ●

SATURDAY № **449** ● / ● /20 ●

SATURDAY № **450** ● / ● /20 ●

SATURDAY № 451 ●/●/20●

SATURDAY № 452 ●/●/20●

SATURDAY nº 453 ●/●/20●

SATURDAY nº 454 ●●/●/20●

SATURDAY № 455 ● / ● /20 ●

SATURDAY № 456 ● / ● /20 ●

SATURDAY № 457 ● /● /20 ●

SATURDAY № 458 ● /● /20 ●

SATURDAY № 459 ● ● / ● /20 ●

SATURDAY № 460 ● ● / ● /20 ●

SATURDAY № 461 ● /● /20 ●

SATURDAY № 462 ● /● /20 ●

SATURDAY n.º 463 ● / ● /20 ●

SATURDAY n.º 464 ● / ● /20 ●

SATURDAY №465 ● /● /20 ●

SATURDAY №466 ● /● /20 ●

SATURDAY № 467 ● / ● /20 ●

SATURDAY № 468 ● / ● /20 ●

SATURDAY № **469** ● / ● /20 ●

SATURDAY № **470** ● / ● /20 ●

SATURDAY № 471 ●/●/20●

SATURDAY № 472 ●/●/20●

SATURDAY № 473  ● / ● /20 ●

SATURDAY № 474  ● / ● /20 ●

SATURDAY № 475 ● / ● /20 ●

SATURDAY № 476 ● / ● /20 ●

SATURDAY № 477 ● / ● /20 ●

SATURDAY № 478 ● / ● /20 ●

SATURDAY № 479 ● / ● /20 ●

SATURDAY № 480 ● / ● /20 ●

SATURDAY № 481  ●/●/20●

SATURDAY № 482  ●/●/20●

SATURDAY № 483 ● / ● /20 ●

SATURDAY № 484 ● / ● /20 ●

SATURDAY №485 ⬤ /⬤ /20 ⬤

SATURDAY №486 ⬤ /⬤ /20 ⬤

SATURDAY № **487** ◐ / ◐ /20 ●

SATURDAY № **488** ◐ / ◐ /20 ●

SATURDAY № 489 ● /● /20 ●

SATURDAY № 490 ● /● /20 ●

SATURDAY №: 491 ● / ● /20 ●

SATURDAY №: 492 ● / ● /20 ●

SATURDAY № 493 ● / ● /20 ●

SATURDAY № 494 ● / ● /20 ●

SATURDAY nº 495 ● / ● /20 ●

SATURDAY nº 496 ● / ● /20 ●

SATURDAY № 497 ● / ● /20 ●

SATURDAY № 498 ● / ● /20 ●

SATURDAY № 499 ● / ● /20 ●

SATURDAY № 500 ● / ● /20 ●

SATURDAY № 501 ● / ● /20 ●

SATURDAY № 502 ● / ● /20 ●

SATURDAY № 503 ● / ● /20 ●

SATURDAY № 504 ● / ● /20 ●

SATURDAY № 505 ● / ● /20 ●

SATURDAY № 506 ● / ● /20 ●

SATURDAY № 507 ● /● /20 ●

SATURDAY № 508 ● /● /20 ●

SATURDAY № 509 ● / ● /20 ●

SATURDAY № 510 ● / ● /20 ●

SATURDAY № 511 ● / ● /20 ●

SATURDAY № 512 ● / ● /20 ●

SATURDAY № 513 ● / ● /20 ●

SATURDAY № 514 ● / ● /20 ●

SATURDAY № 515 ● / ● /20 ●

SATURDAY № 516 ● / ● /20 ●

SATURDAY № 517 ● / ● /20 ●

SATURDAY № 518 ● / ● /20 ●

SATURDAY n⁰ 519 ● / ● /20 ●

SATURDAY n⁰ 520 ● / ● /20 ●

SATURDAY № 521 ● / ● /20 ●

SATURDAY № 522 ● / ● /20 ●

SATURDAY № 523 / /20

SATURDAY № 524 / /20

SATURDAY №º 525 ● / ● /20 ●

SATURDAY №º 526 ● / ● /20 ●

SATURDAY **№ 527** ● / ● /20 ●

SATURDAY **№ 528** ● / ● /20 ●

SATURDAY № 529 ● /● /20 ●

SATURDAY № 530 ● /● /20 ●

SATURDAY № 531 ● / ● /20 ●

SATURDAY № 532 ● / ● /20 ●

SATURDAY № 533 ● / ● /20 ●

SATURDAY № 534 ● / ● /20 ●

SATURDAY № 535 ● / ● /20 ●

SATURDAY № 536 ● / ● /20 ●

SATURDAY № 537 ● / ● /20 ●

SATURDAY № 538 ● / ● /20 ●

SATURDAY № 539 ● / ● /20 ●

SATURDAY № 540 ● / ● /20 ●

SATURDAY **№ 541** ● /● /20 ●

_____

SATURDAY **№ 542** ● /● /20 ●

_____

SATURDAY № 543  ● / ● /20 ●

SATURDAY № 544  ● / ● /20 ●

SATURDAY № 545 ● / ● /20 ●

_____
_____
_____
_____
_____
_____
_____
_____
_____
_____

SATURDAY № 546 ● / ● /20 ●

_____
_____
_____
_____
_____
_____
_____
_____
_____
_____

SATURDAY № 547 ● /● /20 ●

SATURDAY № 548 ● /● /20 ●

SATURDAY № 549 ● / ● /20 ●

SATURDAY № 550 ● / ● /20 ●

SATURDAY nº 551 ⬤ / ⬤ /20 ⬤

SATURDAY nº 552 ⬤ / ⬤ /20 ⬤

SATURDAY № 553 ● / ● /20 ●

SATURDAY № 554 ● / ● /20 ●

SATURDAY № 555 ● / ● /20 ●

SATURDAY № 556 ● / ● /20 ●

SATURDAY № 557 ● / ● /20 ●

SATURDAY № 558 ● / ● /20 ●

SATURDAY № 559 ● / ● /20 ●

SATURDAY № 560 ● / ● /20 ●

SATURDAY № **561** ● / ● /20 ●

SATURDAY № **562** ● / ● /20 ●

SATURDAY № 563 ⬤ / ⬤ /20 ⬤

SATURDAY № 564 ⬤ / ⬤ /20 ⬤

SATURDAY № 565 /  /20

SATURDAY № 566 /  /20

SATURDAY № **567** ⬤ / ⬤ /20 ⬤

SATURDAY № **568** ⬤ / ⬤ /20 ⬤

SATURDAY №569 ● / ● /20 ●

SATURDAY №570 ● / ● /20 ●

SATURDAY №571 ⬤/⬤/20⬤

SATURDAY №572 ⬤/⬤/20⬤

SATURDAY № 573 ● /● /20 ●

SATURDAY № 574 ● /● /20 ●

SATURDAY № 575 ● / ● /20 ●

SATURDAY № 576 ● / ● /20 ●

SATURDAY № 577  ● / ● /20 ●

SATURDAY № 578  ● / ● /20 ●

SATURDAY № 579 ● / ● /20 ●

SATURDAY № 580 ● / ● /20 ●

SATURDAY № 581 ● /● /20 ●

SATURDAY № 582 ● /● /20 ●

SATURDAY № 583 ● /● /20 ●

SATURDAY № 584 ● /● /20 ●

SATURDAY № 585 ● / ● /20 ●

SATURDAY № 586 ● / ● /20 ●

SATURDAY №  587 ●/●/20●

SATURDAY №  588 ●/●/20●

SATURDAY № 589 ● / ● /20 ●

SATURDAY № 590 ● / ● /20 ●

SATURDAY № 591 ● /● /20 ●

SATURDAY № 592 ● /● /20 ●

SATURDAY № 593 ● / ● /20 ●

SATURDAY № 594 ● / ● /20 ●

SATURDAY № 595 ●/●/20●

SATURDAY № 596 ●/●/20●

SATURDAY № 597 ⬤/⬤/20⬤

SATURDAY № 598 ⬤/⬤/20⬤

SATURDAY № 599 ● / ● /20 ●

SATURDAY № 600 ● / ● /20 ●

SATURDAY № 601 ⬤ / ⬤ /20 ⬤

SATURDAY № 602 ⬤ / ⬤ /20 ⬤

SATURDAY № **603**  ● / ● /20 ●

SATURDAY № **604**  ● / ● /20 ●

SATURDAY № 605 ● / ● /20 ●

SATURDAY № 606 ● / ● /20 ●

SATURDAY № 607 ● / ● /20 ●

SATURDAY № 608 ● / ● /20 ●

SATURDAY № 609 ● / ● /20 ●

SATURDAY № 610 ● / ● /20 ●

SATURDAY № 611 ● / ● /20 ●

SATURDAY № 612 ● / ● /20 ●

SATURDAY № 613 ● / ● /20 ●

SATURDAY № 614 ● / ● /20 ●

SATURDAY № 615 ● / ● /20 ●

SATURDAY № 616 ● / ● /20 ●

SATURDAY № **617** ● / ● /20 ●

SATURDAY № **618** ● / ● /20 ●

SATURDAY № **619** ● /● /20●

_____

_____

_____

_____

_____

_____

_____

_____

_____

_____

SATURDAY № **620** ● /● /20●

_____

_____

_____

_____

_____

_____

_____

_____

_____

_____

SATURDAY № 621 ● / ● /20 ●

SATURDAY № 622 ● / ● /20 ●

SATURDAY № 623 ● / ● /20 ●

SATURDAY № 624 ● / ● /20 ●

SATURDAY № 625 ● / ● /20 ●

SATURDAY № 626 ● / ● /20 ●

SATURDAY № 627 ● / ● /20 ●

SATURDAY № 628 ● / ● /20 ●

SATURDAY № 629  ● / ● /20 ●

_____

_____

_____

_____

_____

_____

_____

_____

_____

_____


SATURDAY № 630  ● / ● /20 ●

_____

_____

_____

_____

_____

_____

_____

_____

_____

_____

SATURDAY №631 ⬤ / ⬤ /20 ⬤

SATURDAY №632 ⬤ / ⬤ /20 ⬤

SATURDAY № **633** ● /● /20 ●

_____

SATURDAY № **634** ● /● /20 ●

_____

SATURDAY № **635**      /   /20

SATURDAY № **636**      /   /20

SATURDAY № **637** ● / ● /20 ●

SATURDAY № **638** ● / ● /20 ●

SATURDAY **№ 639** ⬤ / ⬤ /20 ⬤

SATURDAY **№ 640** ⬤ / ⬤ /20 ⬤

SATURDAY № **641** ⬤ / ⬤ /20 ⬤

SATURDAY № **642** ⬤ / ⬤ /20 ⬤

SATURDAY № **643** ● / ● /20 ●

SATURDAY № **644** ● ● /20 ●

SATURDAY № **645** ⬤ / ⬤ /20 ⬤

SATURDAY № **646** ⬤ / ⬤ /20 ⬤

SATURDAY № **647** ● / ● /20 ●

SATURDAY № **648** ● / ● /20 ●

SATURDAY № **649** ● / ● /20 ●

SATURDAY № **650** ● / ● /20 ●

SATURDAY № 651 ● / ● /20 ●

SATURDAY № 652 ● / ● /20 ●

SATURDAY nº 653 ⬤/⬤/20⬤

SATURDAY nº 654 ⬤/⬤/20⬤

SATURDAY №: 655 ● / ● /20 ●

SATURDAY №: 656 ● / ● /20 ●

SATURDAY № **657** ● / ● /20 ●

SATURDAY № **658** ● / ● /20 ●

SATURDAY № **659**  ◖ / ◖ /20 ◗

_____

_____

_____

_____

_____

_____

_____

_____

_____

_____


SATURDAY № **660**  ◖ / ◖ /20 ◗

_____

_____

_____

_____

_____

_____

_____

_____

_____

_____

SATURDAY № **661** ● / ● /20 ●

SATURDAY № **662** ● / ● /20 ●

SATURDAY № **663** ⬤/⬤/20⬤

SATURDAY № **664** ⬤/⬤/20⬤

SATURDAY № 665 ⬤ / ⬤ /20 ⬤

SATURDAY № 666 ⬤ / ⬤ /20 ⬤

SATURDAY № 667 ● / ● /20 ●

SATURDAY № 668 ● / ● /20 ●

SATURDAY № 669 / /20

SATURDAY № 670 / /20

SATURDAY № 671 ● / ● /20 ●

SATURDAY № 672 ● / ● /20 ●

SATURDAY № 673 ● / ● /20 ●

SATURDAY № 674 ● / ● /20 ●

SATURDAY № 675 ● / ● /20 ●

SATURDAY № 676 ● / ● /20 ●

SATURDAY № 677 ● / ● /20 ●

SATURDAY № 678 ● / ● /20 ●

SATURDAY № 679  ● / ● /20 ●

SATURDAY № 680  ● / ● /20 ●

SATURDAY №: **681** ● / ● /20 ●

SATURDAY №: **682** ● / ● /20 ●

SATURDAY № 683 ● / ● /20 ●

SATURDAY № 684 ● / ● /20 ●

SATURDAY №685 ●/●/20●

SATURDAY №686 ●/●/20●

SATURDAY № **687** ● / ● /20 ●

SATURDAY № **688** ● / ● /20 ●

SATURDAY № **689** ● / ● /20 ●

SATURDAY № **690** ● / ● /20 ●

SATURDAY nº 691 ●/●/20●

SATURDAY nº 692 ●/●/20●

SATURDAY № 693  ● / ● /20 ●

_____
_____
_____
_____
_____
_____
_____
_____
_____
_____

SATURDAY № 694  ● / ● /20 ●

_____
_____
_____
_____
_____
_____
_____
_____
_____
_____

SATURDAY № 695 ⬤ / ⬤ /20 ⬤

SATURDAY № 696 ⬤ / ⬤ /20 ⬤

SATURDAY № 697 ● /● /20 ●

SATURDAY № 698 ● /● /20 ●

SATURDAY № 699 ● / ● /20 ●

SATURDAY № 700 ● / ● /20 ●

SATURDAY № 701 ● / ● /20 ●

SATURDAY № 702 ● / ● /20 ●

SATURDAY № **703** ● / ● /20 ●

SATURDAY № **704** ● / ● /20 ●

SATURDAY № 705 ● / ● /20 ●

SATURDAY № 706 ● / ● /20 ●

SATURDAY № 707 ● / ● /20 ●

SATURDAY № 708 ● / ● /20 ●

SATURDAY № 709 ● / ● /20 ●

SATURDAY № 710 ● ● / ● /20 ●

SATURDAY № 713 ● / ● /20 ●

SATURDAY № 714 ● / ● /20 ●

SATURDAY № 715 ● /● /20 ●

SATURDAY № 716 ● /● /20 ●

SATURDAY № 717 ● / ● /20 ●

SATURDAY № 718 ● / ● /20 ●

SATURDAY № 719  ● / ● /20 ●

SATURDAY № 720  ● / ● /20 ●

SATURDAY n.º 721 ● / ● /20 ●

SATURDAY n.º 722 ● / ● /20 ●

SATURDAY № 723 ● / ● /20 ●

SATURDAY № 724 ● / ● /20 ●

SATURDAY № 725　● / ● /20 ●

_____
_____
_____
_____
_____
_____
_____
_____
_____
_____

SATURDAY № 726　● / ● /20 ●

_____
_____
_____
_____
_____
_____
_____
_____
_____
_____

SATURDAY № 727 ● / ● /20 ●

SATURDAY № 728 ● / ● /20 ●

SATURDAY №. 730 ● / ● /20 ●

SATURDAY n⁰ 731 ● /● /20 ●

SATURDAY n⁰ 732 ● /● /20 ●

SATURDAY №733 ● / ● /20 ●

SATURDAY №734 ● / ● /20 ●

SATURDAY №735 ● /● /20 ●

SATURDAY №736 ● /● /20 ●

SATURDAY № 737 ● / ● /20 ●

SATURDAY № 738 ● / ● /20 ●

SATURDAY № 739 ● / ● /20 ●

SATURDAY № 740 ● / ● /20 ●

SATURDAY № 741 ● / ● /20 ●

SATURDAY № 742 ● / ● /20 ●

SATURDAY № 743 ● / ● /20 ●

SATURDAY № 744 ● / ● /20 ●

SATURDAY nº 745 ● /● /20 ●

SATURDAY nº 746 ● /● /20 ●

SATURDAY № 747 ● / ● /20 ●

SATURDAY № 748 ● / ● /20 ●

SATURDAY № 749 ● / ● /20 ●

SATURDAY № 750 ● / ● /20 ●

SATURDAY №️ **751** ⬤ / ⬤ /20 ⬤

SATURDAY №️ **752** ⬤ / ⬤ /20 ⬤

SATURDAY № 753 ●/●/20●

SATURDAY № 754 ●/●/20●

SATURDAY № 755 ●/●/20●

SATURDAY № 756 ●/●/20●

SATURDAY № 757 ● / ● /20 ●

SATURDAY № 758 ● / ● /20 ●

SATURDAY № 759 ⬤/⬤/20⬤

SATURDAY № 760 ⬤/⬤/20⬤

SATURDAY № 761 ● / ● /20 ●

SATURDAY № 762 ● / ● /20 ●

SATURDAY № 763 ● / ● /20 ●

SATURDAY № 764 ● / ● /20 ●

SATURDAY n.º 765 ● / ● /20 ●

SATURDAY n.º 766 ● / ● /20 ●

SATURDAY n⁰ 767 ● / ● /20 ●

SATURDAY n⁰ 768 ● / ● /20 ●

SATURDAY n.º 769 ⬤ / ⬤ /20 ⬤

SATURDAY n.º 770 ⬤ / ⬤ /20 ⬤

SATURDAY № 771 ●/●/20●

SATURDAY № 772 ●/●/20●

SATURDAY № 773 ● / ● /20 ●

SATURDAY № 774 ● / ● /20 ●

SATURDAY № 775 ● / ● /20 ●

SATURDAY № 776 ● / ● /20 ●

SATURDAY nº 777 ● / ● /20 ●

SATURDAY nº 778 ● / ● /20 ●

SATURDAY №: 779 ● / ● /20 ●

SATURDAY №: 780 ● / ● /20 ●

SATURDAY № 781 ●/●/20●

SATURDAY № 782 ●/●/20●

SATURDAY № 783 ● / ● /20 ●

SATURDAY № 784 ● / ● /20 ●

SATURDAY № 785 ● / ● /20 ●

SATURDAY № 786 ● / ● /20 ●

SATURDAY № 787 ● / ● /20 ●

SATURDAY № 788 ● / ● /20 ●

SATURDAY № 789 ● / ● /20 ●

SATURDAY № 790 ● / ● /20 ●

SATURDAY № 791 ● / ● / 20 ●

SATURDAY № 792 ● / ● / 20 ●

SATURDAY № 793 ● /● /20 ●

SATURDAY № 794 ● /● /20 ●

SATURDAY № 795   ● / ● /20●

SATURDAY № 796   ● / ● /20●

SATURDAY N.º 797 ● / ● /20 ●

SATURDAY N.º 798 ● / ● /20 ●

SATURDAY n⁰ 799 ● /● /20●

SATURDAY n⁰ 800 ● /● /20●

SATURDAY № 801  ● / ● /20 ●

SATURDAY № 802  ● / ● /20 ●

SATURDAY №803 / /20

SATURDAY №804 / /20

SATURDAY № **805** ● / ● /20 ●

SATURDAY № **806** ● / ● /20 ●

SATURDAY № **807**  ● / ● /20 ●

SATURDAY № **808**  ● / ● /20 ●

SATURDAY № 809 ● / ● /20 ●

SATURDAY № 810 ● / ● /20 ●

SATURDAY № 811 ● / ● /20 ●

SATURDAY № 812 ● / ● /20 ●

SATURDAY № **813** ● / ● /20 ●

SATURDAY № **814** ● / ● /20 ●

SATURDAY № 815 ⬤/⬤/20⬤

SATURDAY № 816 ⬤/⬤/20⬤

SATURDAY № 817 ● / ● /20 ●

SATURDAY № 818 ● / ● /20 ●

SATURDAY nº 819 ● / ● /20 ●

SATURDAY nº 820 ● / ● /20 ●

SATURDAY № **821** ● / ● /20 ●

SATURDAY № **822** ● / ● /20 ●

SATURDAY № 824 ● /● /20●

SATURDAY № **825** ● / ● /20 ●

SATURDAY № **826** ● / ● /20 ●

SATURDAY nº 827 ● / ● /20 ●

_____

_____

_____

_____

_____

_____

_____

_____

_____

_____

SATURDAY nº 828 ● / ● /20 ●

_____

_____

_____

_____

_____

_____

_____

_____

_____

_____

SATURDAY № **829** ● / ● /20●

SATURDAY № **830** ● / ● /20●

SATURDAY №. 831 ● / ● /20 ●

SATURDAY №. 832 ● / ● /20 ●

SATURDAY № **833** ● / ● /20 ●

SATURDAY № **834** ● / ● /20 ●

SATURDAY № 835 ● / ● /20 ●

SATURDAY № 836 ● / ● /20 ●

SATURDAY № **837** ● / ● /20 ●

SATURDAY № **838** ● / ● /20 ●

SATURDAY № 839　　／　／20

SATURDAY № 840　　／　／20

SATURDAY № 841 ● / ● /20 ●

SATURDAY № 842 ● / ● /20 ●

SATURDAY № 843 ⬤ / ⬤ /20 ⬤

SATURDAY № 844 ⬤ / ⬤ /20 ⬤

SATURDAY **n?** **845** ● /● /20 ●

SATURDAY **n?** **846** ● /● /20 ●

SATURDAY № 847 ● / ● /20 ●

SATURDAY № 848 ● / ● /20 ●

SATURDAY № **849** ● / ● /20 ●

SATURDAY № **850** ● / ● /20 ●

SATURDAY № **851** ● / ● /20 ●

SATURDAY № **852** ● / ● /20 ●

SATURDAY № 853 ● / ● /20 ●

SATURDAY № 854 ● / ● /20 ●

SATURDAY № 855 ⬤ / ⬤ /20 ⬤

SATURDAY № 856 ⬤ / ⬤ /20 ⬤

SATURDAY № **857** ● / ● /20 ●

SATURDAY № **858** ● / ● /20 ●

SATURDAY № **859**  ● / ● /20 ●

SATURDAY № **860**  ● / ● /20 ●

SATURDAY № 861 ● / ● /20 ●

SATURDAY № 862 ● / ● /20 ●

SATURDAY № 863 ● / ● /20 ●

SATURDAY № 864 ● / ● /20 ●

SATURDAY nº 865 ● / ● /20 ●

SATURDAY nº 866 ● / ● /20 ●

SATURDAY № **867** ⬤/⬤/**20**⬤

SATURDAY № **868** ⬤/⬤/**20**⬤

SATURDAY № 869          /     /20

SATURDAY № 870          /     /20

SATURDAY № 871 ● /● /20 ●

SATURDAY № 872 ● /● /20 ●

SATURDAY № 873 ● / ● /20 ●

SATURDAY № 874 ● / ● /20 ●

SATURDAY № 875 ● / ● /20 ●

SATURDAY № 876 ● / ● /20 ●

SATURDAY № **877** ● / ● /20 ●

_____

_____

_____

_____

_____

_____

_____

_____

_____

_____

SATURDAY № **878** ● / ● /20 ●

_____

_____

_____

_____

_____

_____

_____

_____

_____

_____

SATURDAY №. 879 ● /● /20●

SATURDAY №. 880 ● /● /20●

SATURDAY №: **881** ● / ● /20 ●

SATURDAY №: **882** ● / ● /20 ●

SATURDAY № **883**  ● / ● /20 ●

SATURDAY № **884**  ● / ● /20 ●

SATURDAY № 885 ⬤ /⬤ /20 ⬤

SATURDAY № 886 ⬤ /⬤ /20 ⬤

SATURDAY nº 887 ● /● /20 ●

SATURDAY nº 888 ● /● /20 ●

SATURDAY № **889** ● / ● /20 ●

SATURDAY № **890** ● / ● /20 ●

SATURDAY № **891**  ● / ● /20 ●

SATURDAY № **892**  ● / ● /20 ●

SATURDAY № **893** ● / ● /20 ●

_____

_____

_____

_____

_____

_____

_____

_____

_____

SATURDAY № **894** ● / ● /20 ●

_____

_____

_____

_____

_____

_____

_____

_____

_____

SATURDAY №. 895 ● /● /20 ●

_____
_____
_____
_____
_____
_____
_____
_____
_____
_____

SATURDAY №. 896 ● /● /20 ●

_____
_____
_____
_____
_____
_____
_____
_____
_____

SATURDAY nº 897 ● / ● /20 ●

SATURDAY nº 898 ● / ● /20 ●

SATURDAY № 899 ● / ● /20 ●

SATURDAY № 900 ● / ● /20 ●

SATURDAY № 901 ⬤ /⬤ /20⬤

SATURDAY № 902 ⬤ /⬤ /20⬤

SATURDAY № 903 ● / ● /20 ●

SATURDAY № 904 ● / ● /20 ●

SATURDAY № **905** ● / ● /20 ●

SATURDAY № **906** ● / ● /20 ●

SATURDAY №: 907 ● / ● /20 ●

SATURDAY №: 908 ● / ● /20 ●

SATURDAY № 909 ● / ● /20 ●

SATURDAY № 910 ● / ● /20 ●

SATURDAY № 911 ● /● /20 ●

SATURDAY № 912 ● /● /20 ●

SATURDAY № 913 ● / ● /20 ●

SATURDAY № 914 ● / ● /20 ●

SATURDAY № 915 ● / ● /20 ●

SATURDAY № 916 ● / ● /20 ●

SATURDAY № 917 ● / ● /20 ●

SATURDAY № 918 ● / ● /20 ●

SATURDAY № 919 / /20

SATURDAY № 920 / /20

SATURDAY № 921 ●/●/20●

_____
_____
_____
_____
_____
_____
_____
_____
_____
_____

SATURDAY № 922 ●/●/20●

_____
_____
_____
_____
_____
_____
_____
_____
_____
_____

SATURDAY № **923**  ◯ / ◯ /20 ◯

_____
_____
_____
_____
_____
_____
_____
_____
_____
_____

SATURDAY № **924**  ◯ / ◯ /20 ◯

_____
_____
_____
_____
_____
_____
_____
_____
_____
_____

SATURDAY № 925 ⬤ / ⬤ /20 ⬤

SATURDAY №927 ● / ● /20 ●

SATURDAY №928 ● / ● /20 ●

SATURDAY n.º 929 ● / ● /20 ●

SATURDAY n.º 930 ● / ● /20 ●

SATURDAY № 931 ● / ● /20 ●

SATURDAY № 932 ● / ● /20 ●

SATURDAY №: 933 ● /● /20●

SATURDAY №: 934 ● /● /20●

SATURDAY № 935  ● / ● /20 ●

SATURDAY № 936  ● / ● /20 ●

SATURDAY № 937 ● / ● /20 ●

SATURDAY № 938 ● / ● /20 ●

SATURDAY № 939 ● / ● /20 ●

SATURDAY № 940 ● / ● /20 ●

# MILESTONES

## Saturday 1

"Now what do we do?!" The first Saturday at home with your new baby is like no other Saturday of your life. Most of the day is spent watching, wondering, and worrying.

The uncertainty and insecurity of Saturday 1 is humbling and unsettling. How could someone like you, so accomplished and self-confident in other situations, be so flummoxed and flabbergasted by this 8-pound bundle of bliss? How did *other parents* figure it out? Who taught *them*? How did *their* babies survive infancy and make it to the tricycle they're riding (and, by the way, shouldn't that kid be wearing a helmet!)? Surely there must be an app for getting from Saturday 1 to Saturday 2!

Yes, it is anxiety provoking and awe inspiring, but you WILL get through it and your child will ride a tricycle someday, too (with a helmet!). By the time he's riding a tricycle, though, you will already be at Saturday 156! So what are you waiting for? Start journaling now, lest the memories of these wondrous moments get lost in the chaos.

## Saturdays 2–939: Your Child's Developmental Milestones

Child development is a continuum, a gentle ramp or incline, not a series of discrete steps on a staircase. Although the differences between a 6-month-old and a 6-year-old are dramatic, the differences between a 5-year-old and a 6-year-old are much less so.

"Milestone madness" is a common derangement among parents of young kids who compare their kids to others or overanalyze a summary of developmental milestones like the one below. I've assembled the following overview of what you can expect from your child's body, brain, and behavior during Saturdays 2–939 to give you a better understanding of the wondrous growth and development that form the basis for the activities in the booklet. Of course, if you have concerns about your child's developmental progress, speak with his doctor—but don't obsess about the timing. Kids find their own pace.

## Birth–2 Years / SATURDAYS 2–104

These are the halcyon Stroller Saturdays, when a simple walk in the park brings contentment to you and your baby. But, between strolls, there's so much more fun to be had. Your baby is about to turn from blob to blabbermouth—don't miss a word!

## Birth–1 Month

**BODY** • Moves arms and legs randomly • moves head side to side when lying on stomach • has sucking, rooting reflexes • grasps your finger • holds his hands in tight fists

**BRAIN** • Has mature hearing • startles to loud noises • is comforted by soft sounds • reacts to light, voice, feeding • focuses on your face • recognizes the smell of mother's milk

**BEHAVIOR** • Sleeps much of the day • prefers mother's voice • responds to rocking and cuddling • cries to show discomfort and hunger

## 1 Month–3 Months

**BODY** • Lifts head when lying on stomach • has less head lag when pulled to sit • holds a rattle • swipes at dangling objects • holds hands open or with loose fists

**BRAIN** • Follows a toy with eyes • looks at own fingers • recognizes you • turns head to bright lights, bold colors, distinctive sounds • concentrates on mobiles • notices patterns

**BEHAVIOR** • Is awake longer • waves arms and kicks legs for communication • gets excited at feeding and bathing • cries to bring you running, stops when you pick him up • smiles responsively • "talks back" to you with noises • coos, laughs, gurgles

## 3 Months–6 Months

**BODY** • Has head control • sits with support • rolls back to side, then front to side, then front to back • shakes a rattle • grasps objects with palm • holds a toy with two hands • puts food in mouth • pulls toes (and everything else) to mouth • splashes in bath • bounces when held standing

**BRAIN** • Distinguishes between different colors, tastes, smells • focuses on toys and mirror • follows with eyes and head • recognizes your voice • babbles single syllables (*da-da-da-da*) • imitates sounds • plays with interactive toys • plays peek-a-boo

**BEHAVIOR** • Shows curiosity and concentration • smiles at own face in mirror • giggles, squeals • communicates with sounds, facial expressions • is affectionate to parents, friendly to others

## 6 Months–1 Year

**BODY** • Rolls back to front • rolls across the room • sits unsupported • reaches for objects while sitting • transfers objects from one hand to the other • bangs objects together • puts objects in containers • creeps and crawls (including up and down stairs) • pulls to stand • cruises around furniture • stands without support • walks with support • sits up from lying and sits down from standing • waves bye-bye • claps • points • makes marks with a large crayon • picks up small objects between thumb and forefinger • finger-feeds Cheerios • holds spoon, cup, bottle • drinks from a sippy cup

**BRAIN** • Concentrates on pictures and objects • learns "permanence" (a dropped spoon isn't lost forever!) • recognizes own name and a few words • responds to "no" (enjoy it while it lasts!) • localizes sounds • points to body parts • likes new foods and textures • plays patty-cake • combines sounds • speaks first word(s) • shouts for attention • likes television (uh-oh!) and music

**BEHAVIOR** • Has stranger and separation anxiety • may be shy • communicates with gestures • holds up arms to be picked up • cuddles • resists sharing toys • protests

## 1 Year–18 Months

**BODY** • Walks without support • climbs into chairs • "fetches" rolling balls • stacks cubes • pounds pegs in workbench • scribbles with crayons • uses a spoon • drinks from a regular cup • turns thick book pages

**BRAIN** • Has mature eyesight • follows others' movements closely • concentrates on storybooks • points to named objects • follows simple instructions • speaks a few words and word combinations • mimics animal sounds ("What does a cat say?" "Meow!")

**BEHAVIOR** • Explores every corner, closet, container • may have security toy or blanket • may be fearful of some things (e.g., dogs, loud vacuum cleaners) • shows more nuanced emotions (jealousy, anxiety) • may be moody at times

## 18 Months–2 Years

**BODY** • Walks more confidently • runs a bit • kneels • dances and marches to music • climbs stairs and everywhere else (up better than down; caution: can climb out of crib!) • throws a ball underhand • kicks a large ball • builds 3- to 5-block towers • demonstrates hand preference • turns thin book pages • uses a toy hammer • assembles lift-out puzzles • scribbles with pencils • may be ready to start potty training • pounds and rolls clay • strings spools and beads

**BRAIN** • Names objects • follows two-step instructions • echoes words • has vocabulary of 50 or more words • uses "Tarzan speech" ("Me eat cookie") • understands easy questions • remembers places • laughs at silly and slapstick humor

**BEHAVIOR** • Asks for food, potty, toys • pulls you to show you things • shows independence and frustration • may have tantrums • "helps" around the house • may display aggressive behavior • has short attention span • bolts away from you (caution!)

## 2-5 Years | SATURDAYS 105-260

Toddler and preschool Saturdays are exciting times when your child has matured from fragile to agile, wary to daring. The variety of weekend adventures grows exponentially along with your child during these years, and will become her first lifelong memories.

## 2–3 Years

**BODY** • Runs • climbs up and down stairs without holding on • climbs on playground and slides • enjoys ride-on toys (feet on ground) • catches a large ball with two hands • throws a small ball overhand • builds 6- to 8-block towers • turns knobs, opens boxes, unscrews lids and unwraps packages • opens doors • bangs with sticks on drum, xylophone, and siblings • holds crayon well • copies shapes when drawing • feeds self • undresses mittens and socks • puts on shoes (not laces) • may have completed daytime potty training

**BRAIN** • Sorts by shape, color, size • recognizes people in photographs • understands many words • listens to conversations • concentrates on details in books • speaks short phrases, sentences, questions • has vocabulary of 200 or more words • follows two-step instructions • understands "now" and "later" • names body parts and colors • knows nursery rhymes • recognizes patterns • may recognize letter combinations (e.g., his name, "STOP")

**BEHAVIOR** • Engages in imaginative play • plays beside (but not with) others • demonstrates nurturing play (cares for stuffed animals, dolls) • narrates his own play aloud • says "no" in protest (a lot!) • may have more frequent tantrums • may take turns in a game but very possessive of toys • earns "time outs" • is ready for first bed

## 3–4 Years

**BODY** • Jumps • stands and hops on one foot • navigates more sophisticated playground equipment • rides tricycle or bicycle with training wheels • builds 10-block towers, 3-block bridges • puts on pants, socks • buttons clothes • kicks a ball forward • keeps self going on swing • uses a fork • threads large beads • sculpts occasionally recognizable shapes • uses child-safe scissors • brushes teeth with help • has nighttime bowel and bladder control

**BRAIN** • Has vocabulary of 1,000 words • speaks longer and more complicated sentences • tells short stories • understands "before/after," "same/different" • follows multistep instructions • puts toys on shelf, laundry in hamper • clears dishes from the table • names shapes, colors, letters • counts a few objects

**BEHAVIOR** • Asks constant questions • forms permanent memories • chats with you and friends • has somewhat better control of emotions • negotiates solutions to conflicts • engages in social play, shares, takes turns • listens to suggestions and follows instructions • shows kindness and concern • may confuse make-believe for reality • is less clingy, more independent

## 4–5 Years

**BODY** • Skips • somersaults • swings • climbs trees • catches a small ball • swings a tennis racket and baseball bat • pours water into cups • paints with large and medium brushes • has adult pencil grip • eats with knife and fork

**BRAIN** • Recognizes capital letters • concentrates on small puzzles • holds conversations • tells long stories • enjoys rhyming • counts 10 or more objects • has vocabulary of 1,500 words • understands "yesterday/today/tomorrow" • may be able to download apps (caution!) • prints letters • draws a house, figures with body parts

**BEHAVIOR** • Wants friends to like him • plays games with friends and follows rules • is more patient but still can be emotional • alternates between being resistant and cooperative • begins to consider needs of others • comforts friends • likes to "perform" for others • distinguishes make-believe from reality

---

## 5 to 11    5–11 Years / SATURDAYS 261–572

Your "baby" is now in kindergarten or grade school and acquiring many adult skill sets. Make the most of his new abilities with stimulating family Saturdays.

---

## 5–7 Years

**BODY** • Writes name • walks and runs like an adult • can walk backward • loves playing tag • balances on one leg for 10 seconds or longer • walks a balance beam • combines simple movements (run *and* kick, jump *and* twist) • jumps a rope turned by others • uses tools (hammer, screwdriver) • dresses quickly • ties shoes • uses computer keyboard well • may ride a two-wheeler • throws a ball well both over- and underhand • hits a ball off a tee • dribbles a basketball

**BRAIN** • Draws multi-item realistic pictures • speaks fluently with complex sentences • learns to measure • tells time • enjoys putting things together and taking them apart • increases vocabulary from 5,000 words to 10,000 or more (learns 10–20 new words each day!) • writes upper- and lowercase alphabet letters • spells short words, "invents" spelling of others • has good counting skills (forward and backward) • estimates numbers of objects • performs simple addition and subtraction • makes art designs, combines different art mediums • appreciates music, sings many songs • "acts" in shows

**BEHAVIOR** • Plays well alone and with others • seeks friendships and acceptance • relates well to adults • shows compassion • acts calmer and more mature, good self-control • compromises and negotiates to solve conflicts • comforts self • takes turns in conversations • may exaggerate feelings ("Everybody hates me!") • believes rules can be changed • has high energy, rarely tired

## 7–9 Years

**BODY** • Rides a two-wheeler • has increased strength and endurance, better hand-eye coordination • combines complex athletic movements (runs *and* dribbles, jumps *and* catches, dives *and* blocks) • kicks and throws accurately and forcefully • may be able to do cartwheels, handstands • jumps a self-turned rope • hits objects in motion with a bat, hockey stick, tennis racket

**BRAIN** • Increased attention span for learning new things • uses logic to solve problems and riddles • is more organized, able to "declutter" closets and drawers (but probably won't!) • creates expressive art • maintains tunes on musical instruments • sight-reads many words, sounds out others • reads fluently aloud • summarizes stories • writes complete sentences with good grammar and spelling of simple words • uses a dictionary • counts to 200 or higher • counts by 5s • solves simple word problems

**BEHAVIOR** • Joins organized clubs and teams, has good social skills and sportsmanship • is attentive to rules in games and sports • may become competitive • may mask true feelings to protect others' feelings • alternates between self-confidence and self-criticism • likes consistency, resists change • may have decreased appetite • prefers playmates of same sex • has a "best friend" • requests responsibilities • may show aggressiveness • is forgetful, distractible •

exhibits maturing emotions (guilt, shame) • may be secretive, private, and modest (e.g., has secret conversations with friends, keeps a "private" diary, resists being seen naked)

## 9–11 Years

**BODY** • Exhibits slow and steady physical growth leading to puberty growth spurt • has "growing pains" • runs faster and jumps higher • improves balance and agility • has improved handwriting

**BRAIN** • Thinks concretely, focuses on rules, classifies, categorizes • has longer attention span for classroom learning • begins to hypothesize • understands sarcasm • develops spatial reasoning (draws maps, estimates distances) • draws with depth perspective • has much improved fine-motor skills • creates complex craft projects • touch-types on keyboard • plays complex video and computer games • plans ahead, shows anticipatory thinking • establishes and pursues goals

**BEHAVIOR** • May be cliquish • may emerge as a group leader or follower • forms more complex friendships • closes bedroom door for privacy • seeks peer approval • develops "crushes" • has better emotional regulation and awareness of appropriate behavior • understands and experiences mixed emotions • bases self-image on how he thinks peers perceive him • experiments with music and other skills requiring lessons • negotiates rules with parents

**11–14 Years / SATURDAYS 573–728**

The "tween" and middle-school years present unique challenges for kids and parents, and unique opportunities as well. Different rates of physical and emotional maturity can be stressful for everyone. Meaningful weekends together set the tone for healthy and happy development.

**BODY** • PUBERTY! • has dramatic weight and height gain • may be physically awkward (bones grow faster than muscles) • is always hungry • develops acne • has sharpened motor skills and athletic abilities • may be better at sports than parents

**BRAIN** • Develops analytical thinking and logical arguments • considers different hypotheses to explain things • is reflective • seeks solutions to real-life problems • has better organizational skills and work habits (or not!) • is eager to try new things (new talents emerge!) • is aware of own limitations • formulates mature goals

**BEHAVIOR** • Develops heightened concern with appearance • may be embarrassed by physical changes • has emerging sense of sexuality • struggles between wanting independence and seeking parental input • may challenge authority (warning: it gets worse later!) • has periods of restlessness and listlessness • needs to conform with, and be accepted by, peers • can be insensitive and mean to those outside clique • may be more opinionated • becomes idealistic with strong sense of "right" and "wrong" • demonstrates emotional ups and downs, angry or aggressive outbursts, inconsistent and erratic actions • may be introspective and very sensitive to criticism • personalizes others' actions • requires frequent affirmation by adults • adopts celebrities and sports heroes as role models

**14 to 18**

Teens' brains are incompletely developed until late adolescence (or well beyond!), leading to potential conflicts in school and at home. It's easy to fall into the "parent-of-adolescents trap" and believe your kids would rather hang with anyone but you (and, indeed, they might!). But, as you'll see in the Activities booklet, there are many tricks to lure even the coolest high schoolers into spending memorable family time.

**BODY** • Puberty continues • exhibits rapid growth in height, weight, strength • requires 9–10 hours sleep • may be clumsy • is always *"starving"* (needs more calories) • is able to master new physical challenges • develops adult physique and physical abilities

**BRAIN** • Has advanced reasoning skills (but may not use them!) • thinks more logically and hypothetically ("What if . . .") • hones in on inconsistencies in rules and behavior • exhibits abstract thinking (e.g., spirituality, morals, values, philosophical concepts) • seeks self-identity

**BEHAVIOR** • May be overly dramatic • is inconsistent in controlling emotions • may have poor judgment • may be rebellious, argumentative, elusive • is self-conscious, embarrassed to be seen with parents • may have sense of invulnerability leading to risky behavior • may be sensitive about weight gain and dieting, may develop unhealthy eating habits • is awkward regarding discussions of sex • seeks intimacy with others (including sexual relationships) • spends more time with friends than with family • may become obsessive (or neglectful) about clothes, grooming, skin care • adopts social causes • has rapidly changing interests and passions

## Saturday 940

Phew! That was a hypersonic tour through childhood. For most of you journaling the Saturdays with your kids, Saturday 940 is a distant destination. But it arrives faster than you realize, and it's another truly extraordinary parenting moment when it does. The time to begin anticipating Saturday 940, and making sure you're emotionally ready, is now, when your kids are still young. It's how you spend time in the present that brings the satisfaction and fulfillment you'll feel when Saturday 940 rolls around.

Which brings me to a word about guilt. Lose it! Okay, that's two words. But my point is simple: there may be many Saturdays along the way when it's impossible to do what you had planned with your kids because life gets in the way. If you're trying as hard as you can to share as many of the *940 Saturdays* as possible with your kids, striving to make those weekends memorable, you can't feel guilty about the inevitable impossible Saturdays. *940 Saturdays* is a guilt-buster, tangible evidence of your awesome parenting.

So, are you ready for Saturday 940? Of course not! But by taking advantage of the hundreds of activities in the accompanying booklet, and journaling your family's Saturday memories, you're well on your way to being ready when the time comes. In the meantime, enjoy every fabulous moment!